SHE HELD HER BREATH IN WONDER

She Held Her Breath in Wonder

a story of Maria Sibylla Merian

PAIGE MENTON

Samantha Holden

Journeywork Press

We wish to thank Natalia Koninina for all of her expert help with layout.

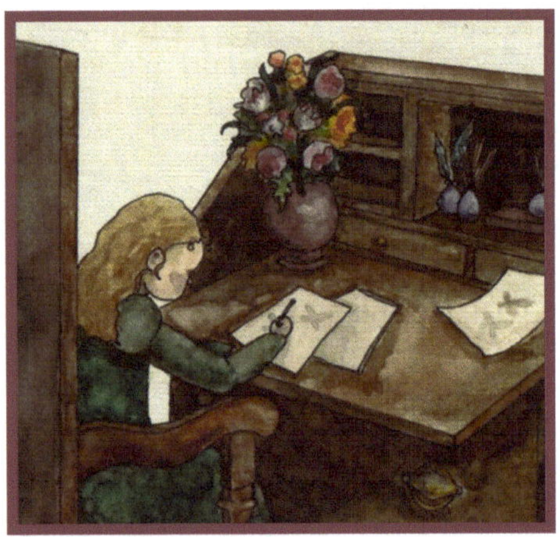

First Journeywork Press edition 2023

The text for this book was hand sewn with embroidery thread.

ISBN 979-8-218-14926-0

To Michael, Christopher, and Manya
- Paige

To my family, for their unwavering support
- Samantha

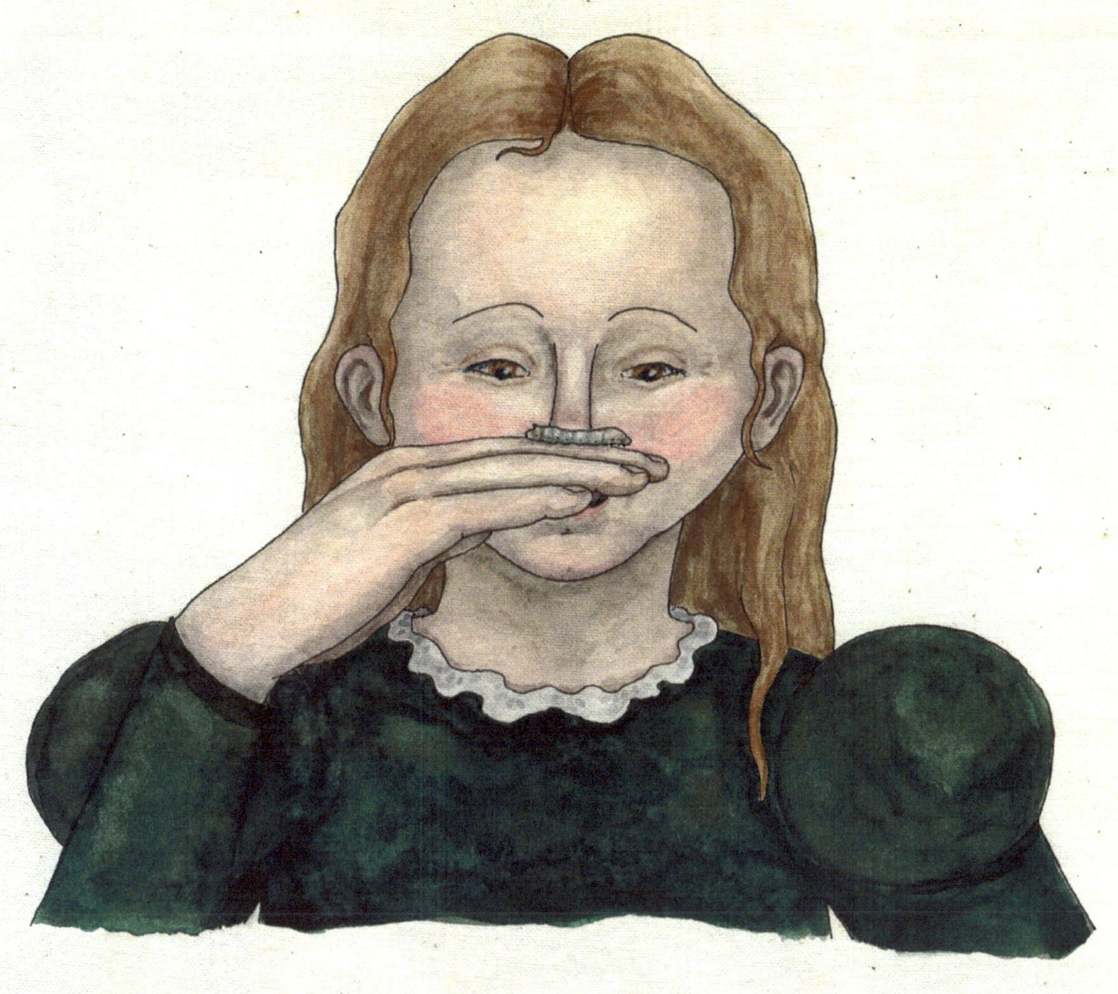

When Maria Sibylla Merian was a girl,
she received a gift of silkworms.

The adults around her did not
know much about silkworms,
Maria fed her pets mulberry leaves,
watched them spin their cocoons,
and kept them in boxes until they
emerged as moths.

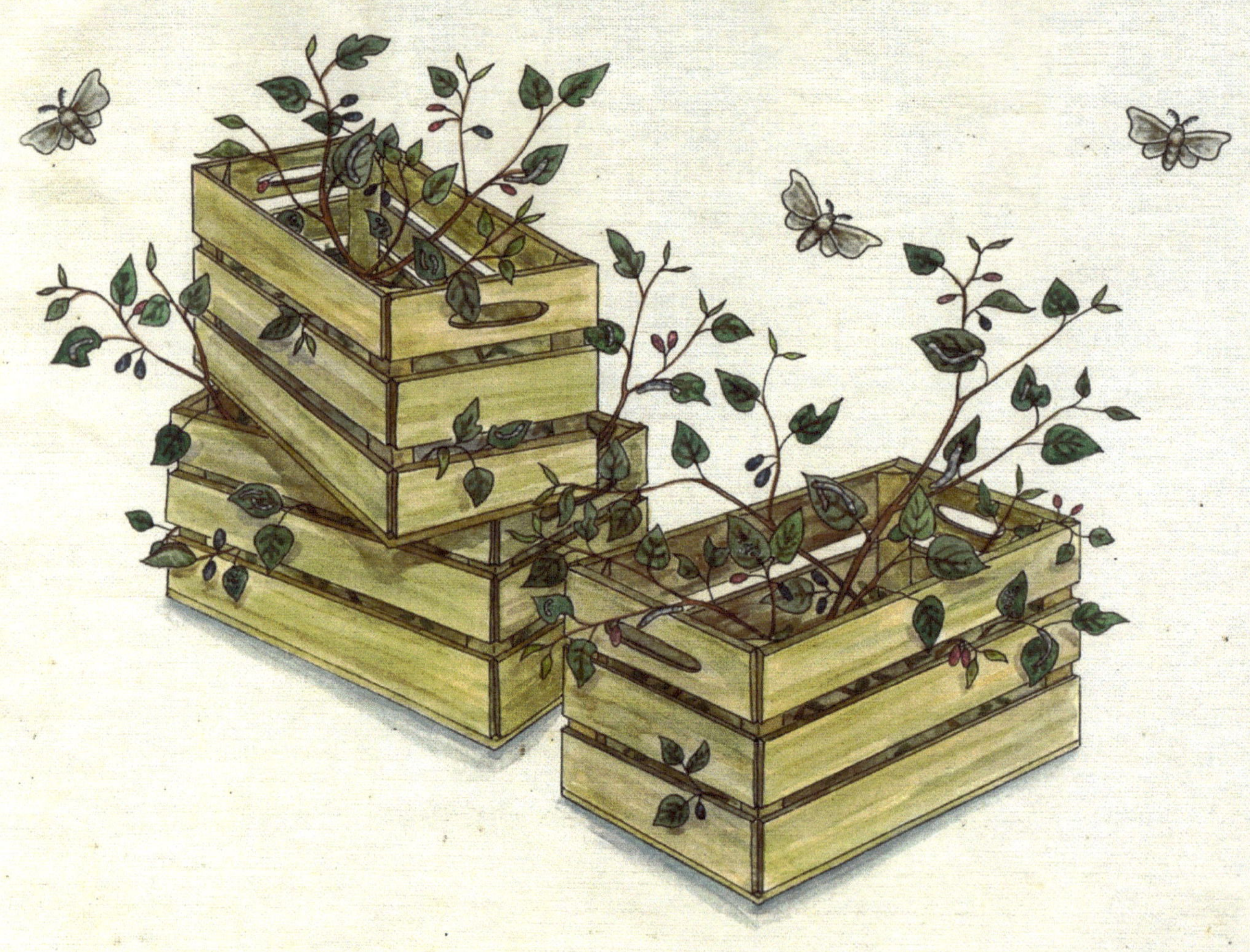

Maria drew each stage of the moth's life on the first page of a sketchbook that she would use for the rest of her life.

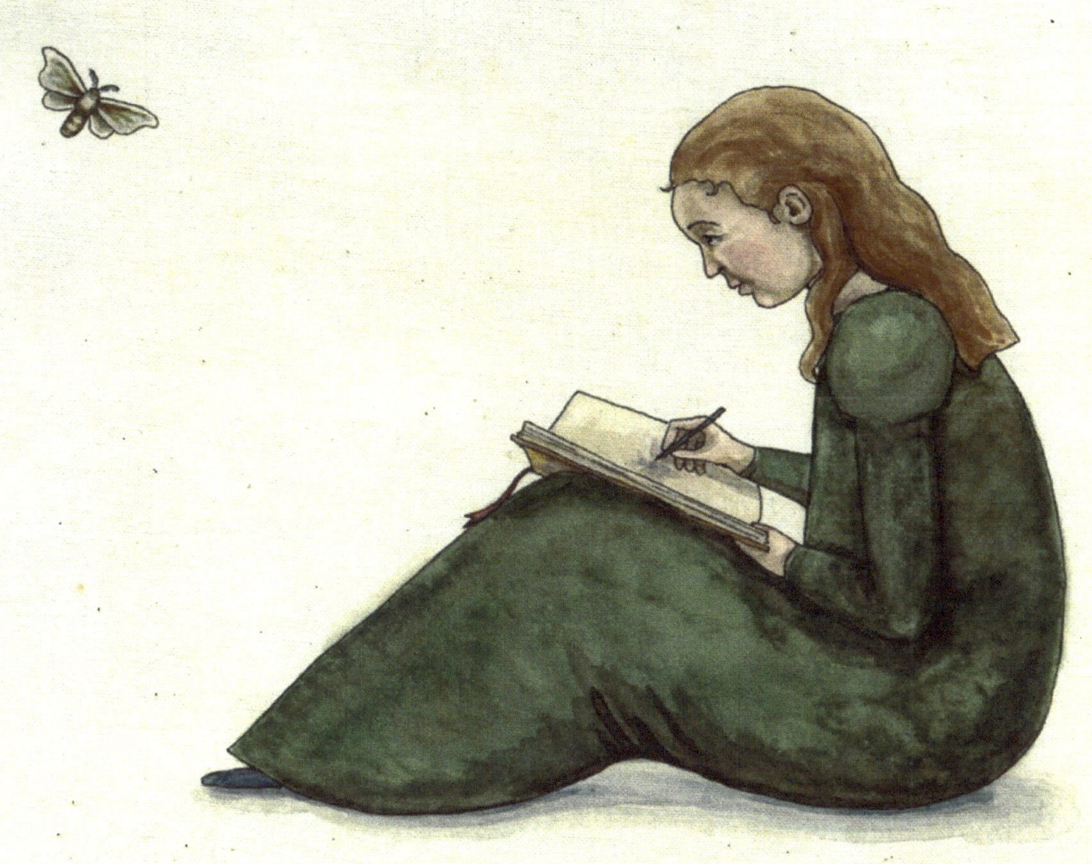

Maria understood how silkworms become moths when she was thirteen years old, nine years before the leading scientists of the day.

Maria was thirteen in 1660.

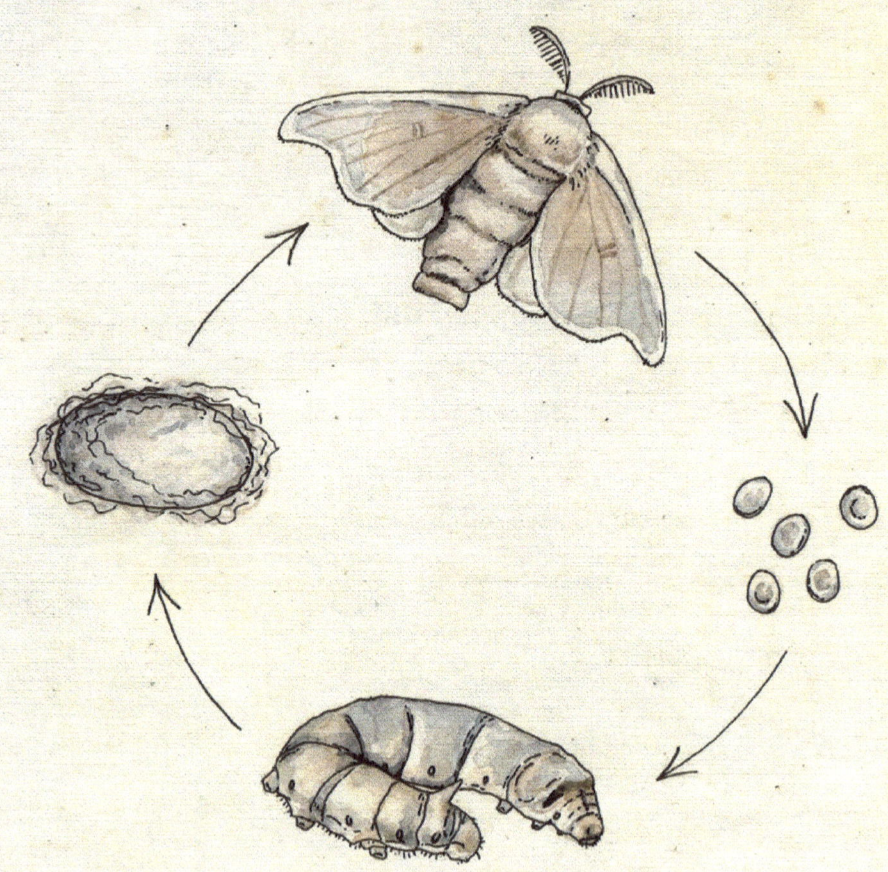

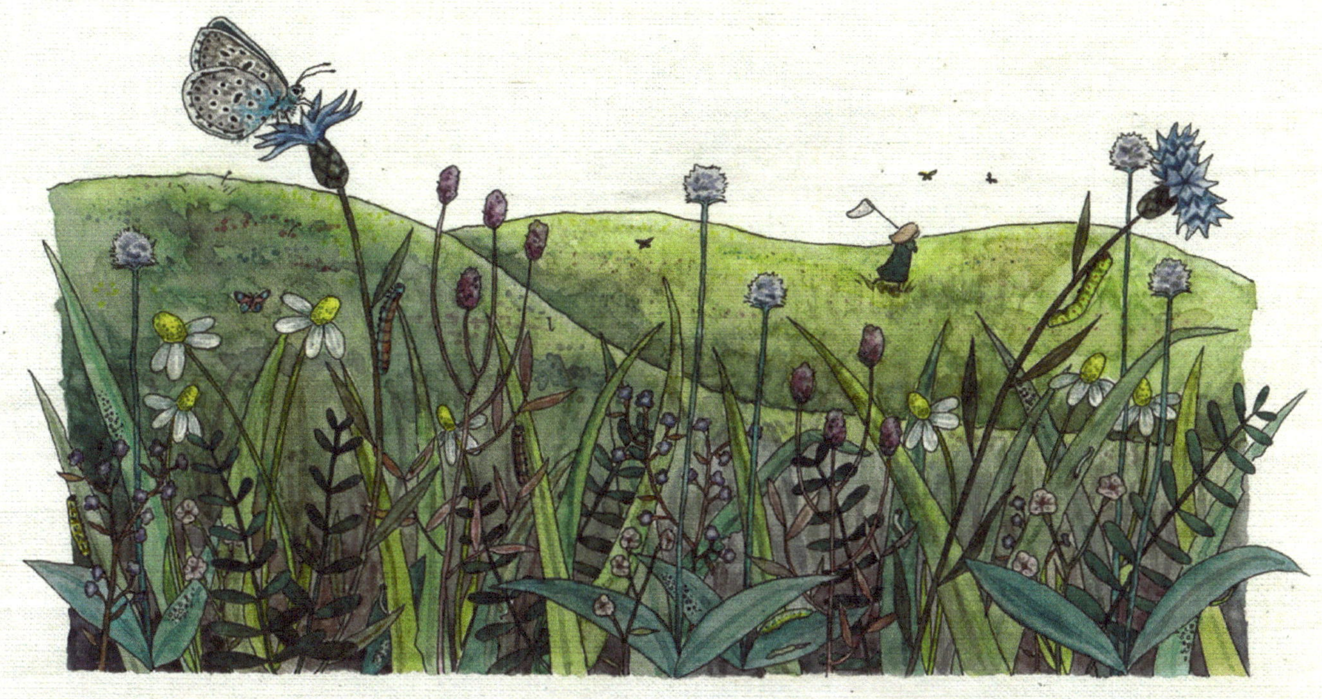

Maria scoured the fields around
her house in Frankfurt, Germany
for butterflies and moths. She
searched for butterfly eggs under
the leaves of her mother's flowers.

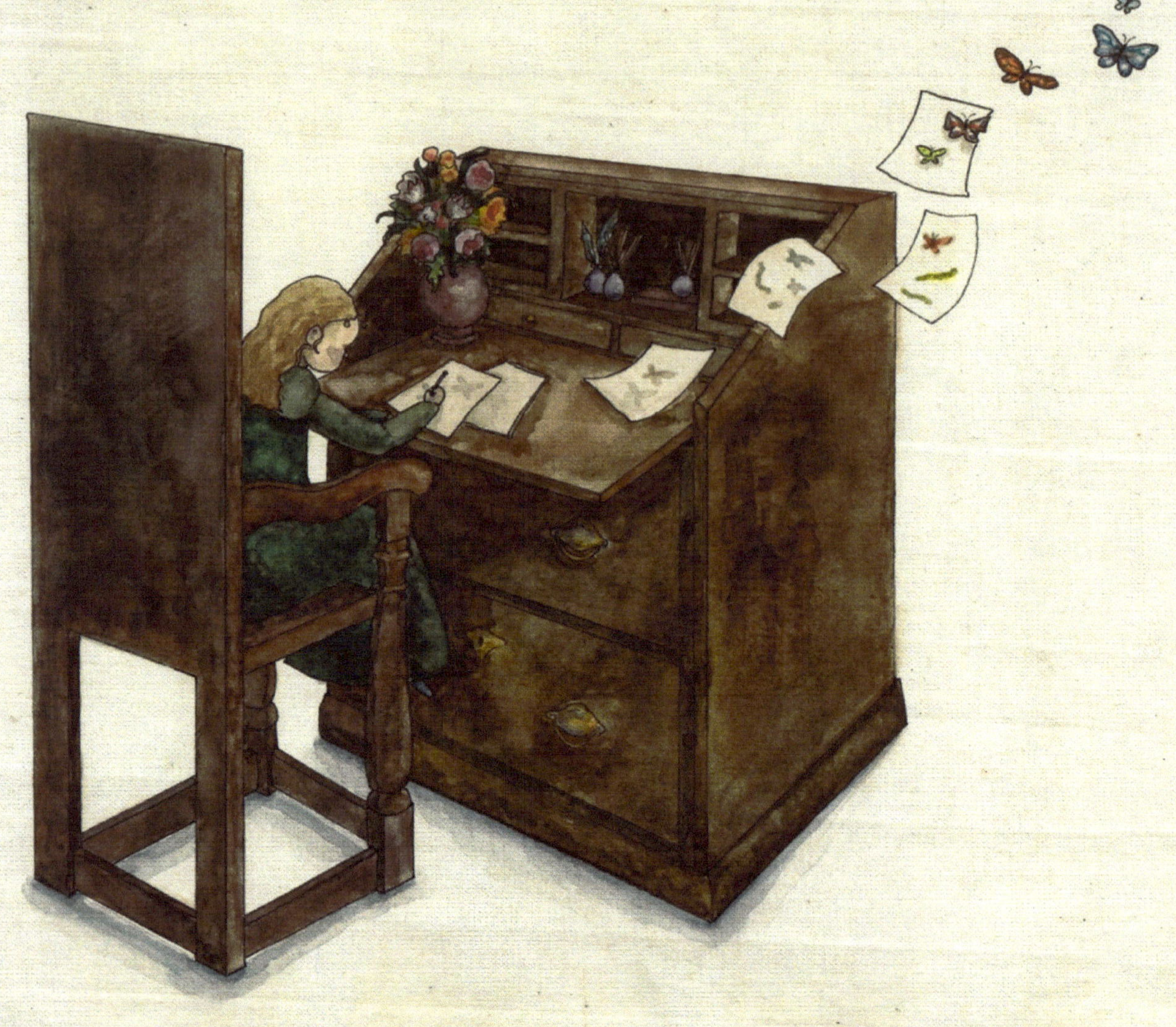

And Maria drew. She raised all the kinds of butterflies she could find, and she drew them in all of the stages she could see.

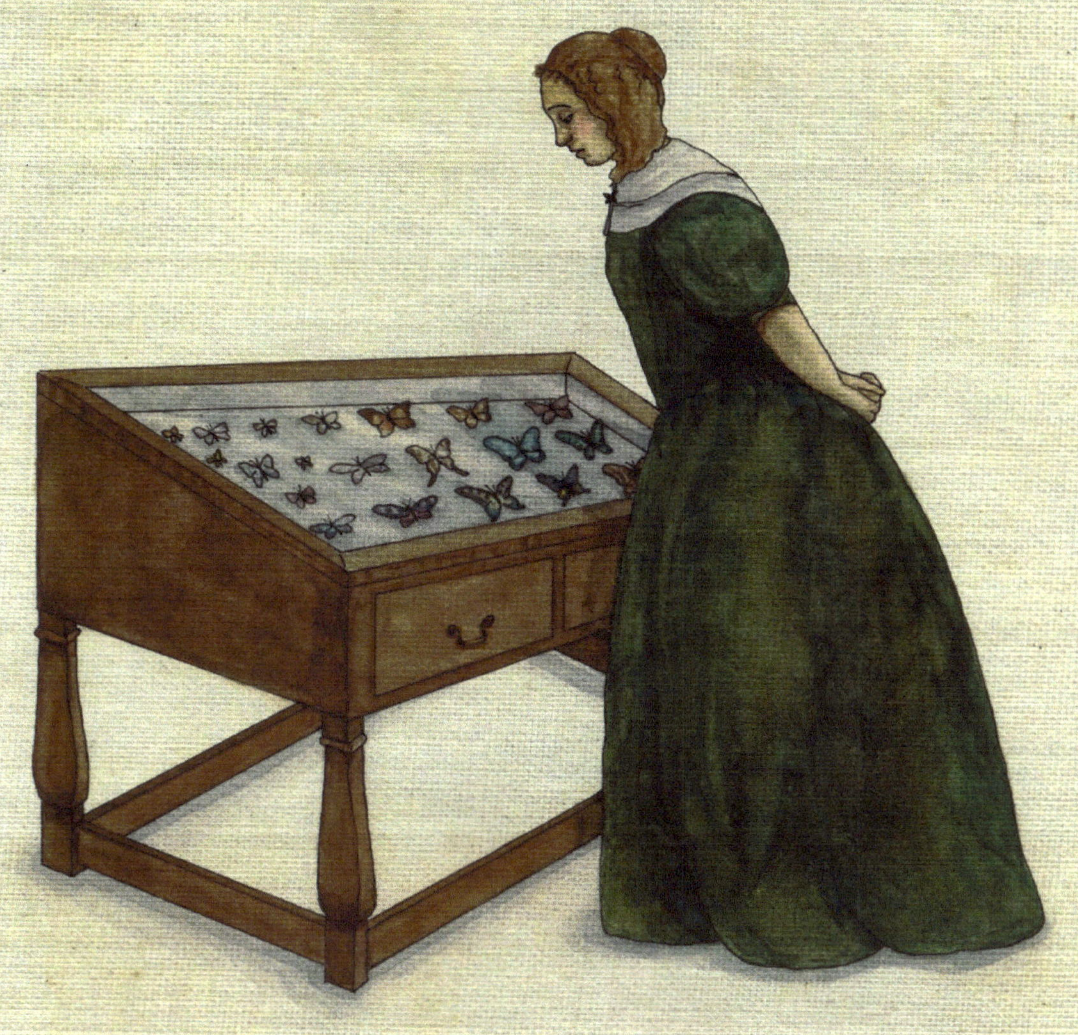

Maria grew up and moved to
Amsterdam. She saw butterflies
she had never seen before, but
they were pinned down in cases.

Wealthy people collected plants and animals from the Americas. They built curiosity cabinets to hold their treasures, and they hired Maria to draw them.

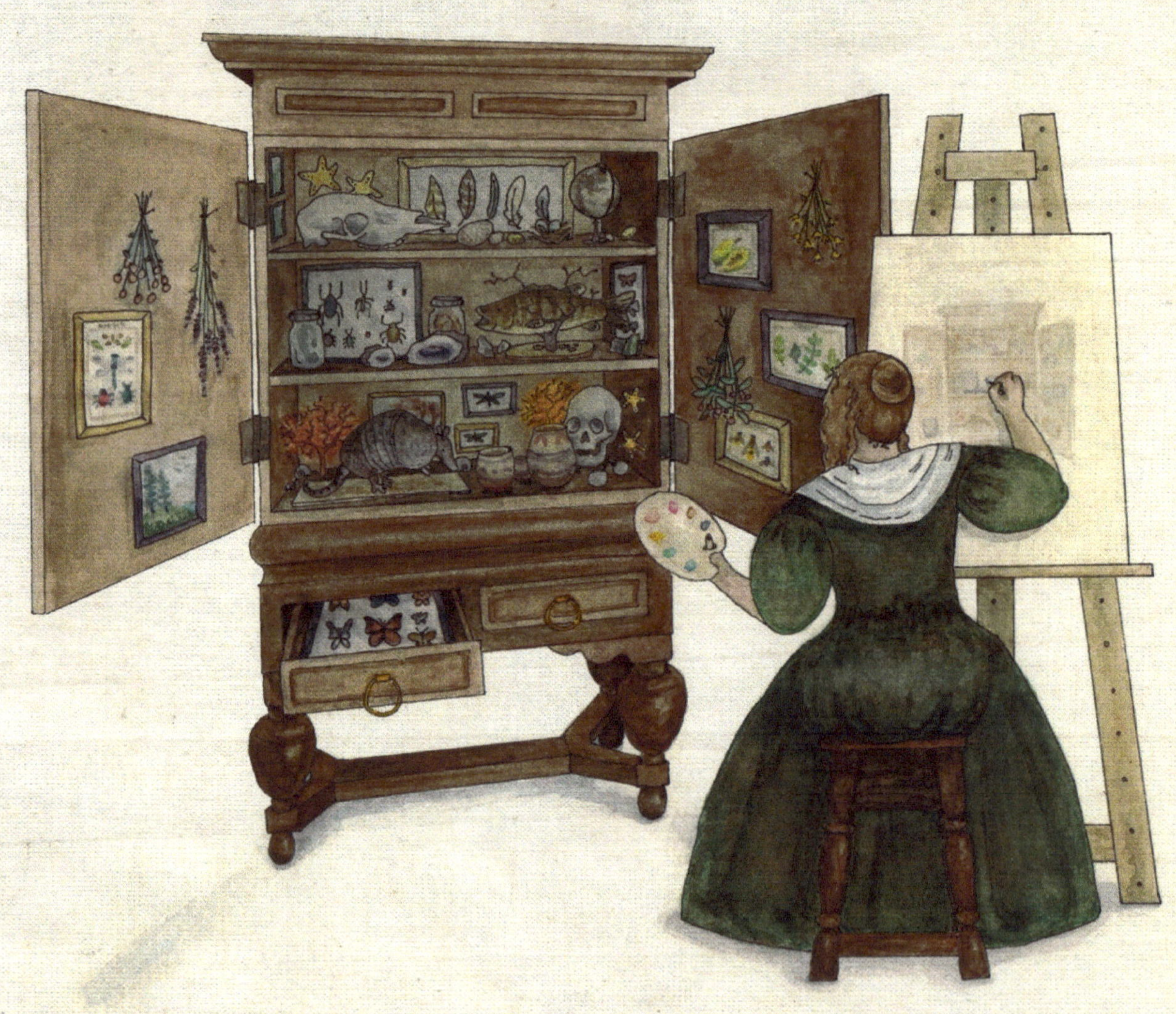

Curious Maria could not bear to see these lifeless butterflies without knowing what they ate and where they lived.

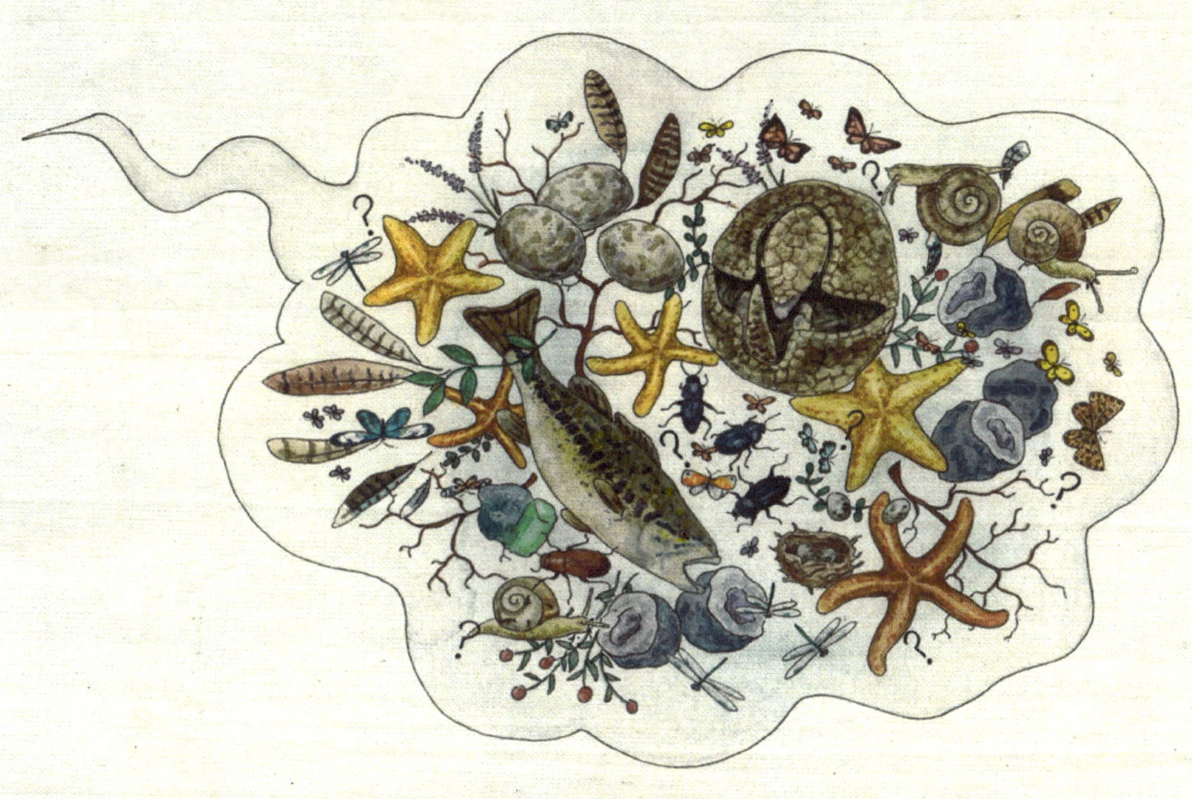

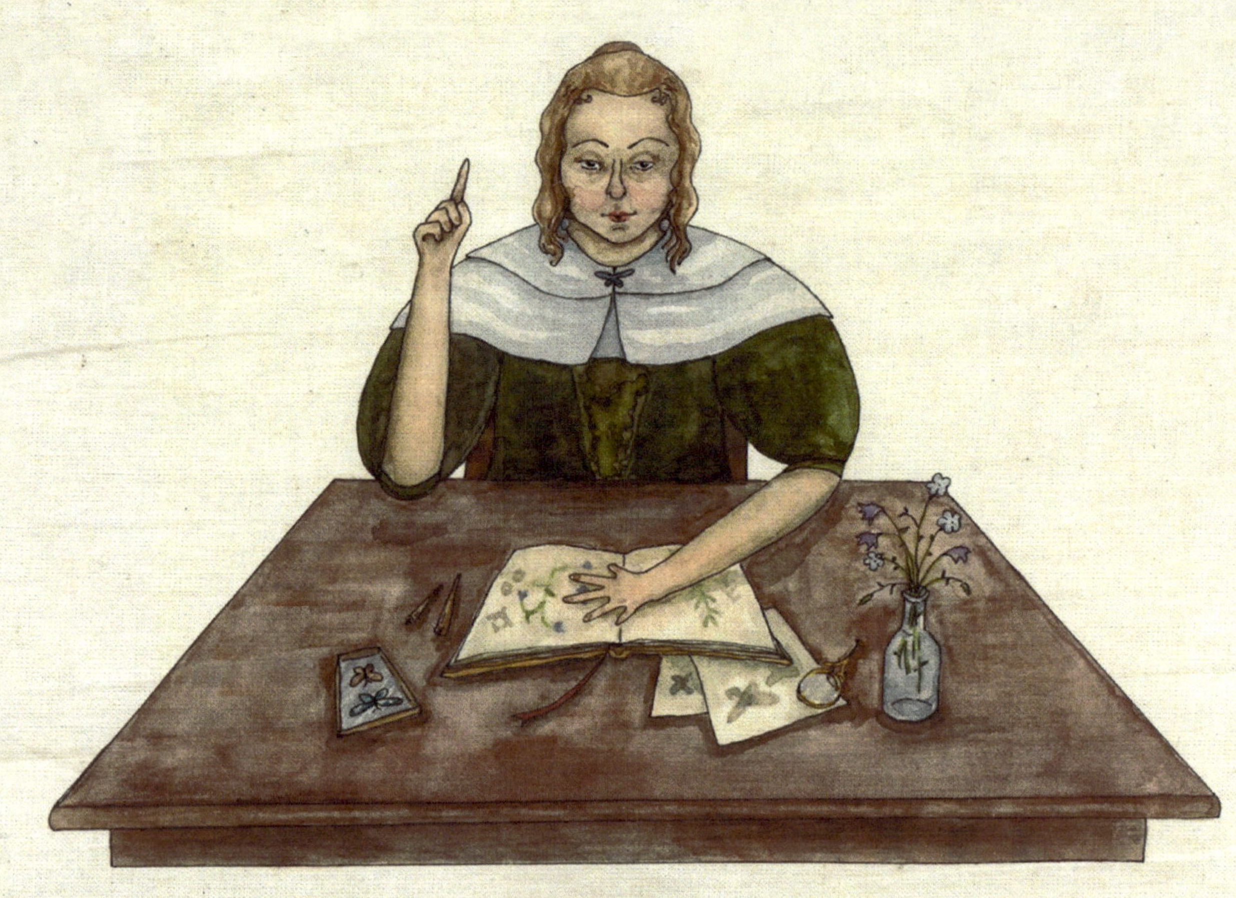

Maria had an idea. She would make a book. The book would be full of butterflies, painted as they lived with the plants that their caterpillars ate.

There was no book like this.
Most of the books about the
Americas had pictures of
giant sea serpents. The people
in Europe thought that these
monsters were real.

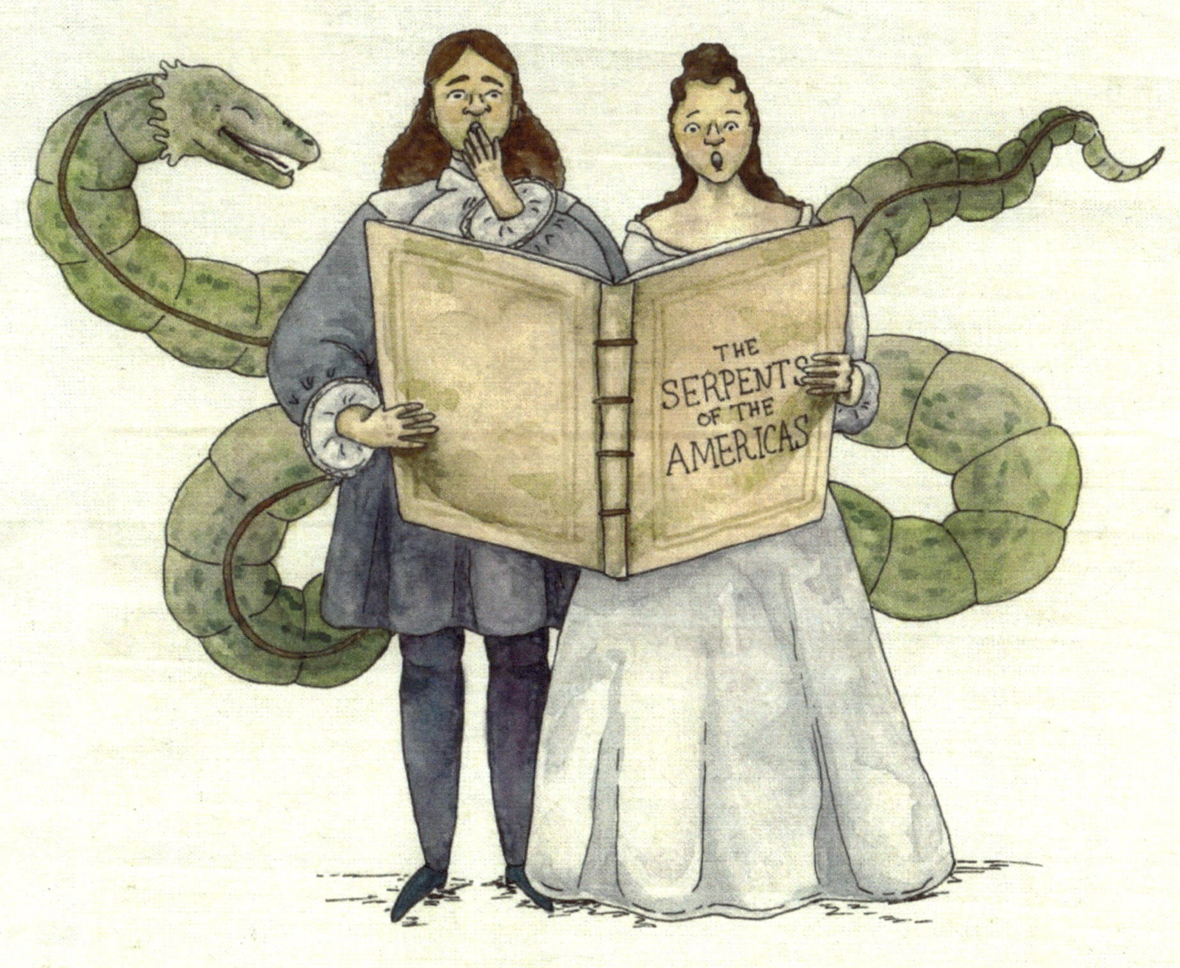

Very few men voyaged to the
Americas to draw the plants and
animals there, and no woman
from Europe had ever gone. Maria
would travel to the Americas
and draw exactly what she saw.

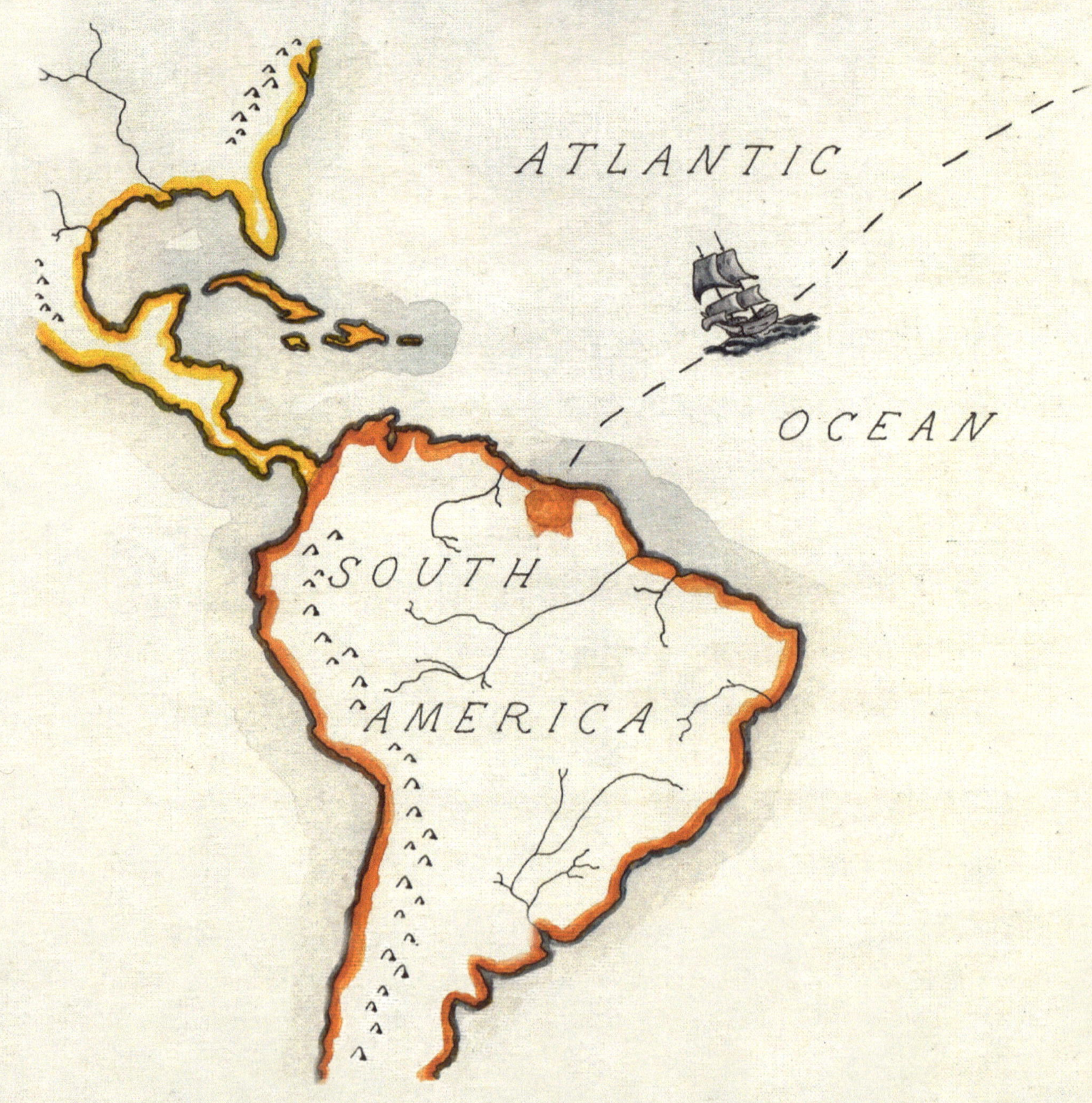

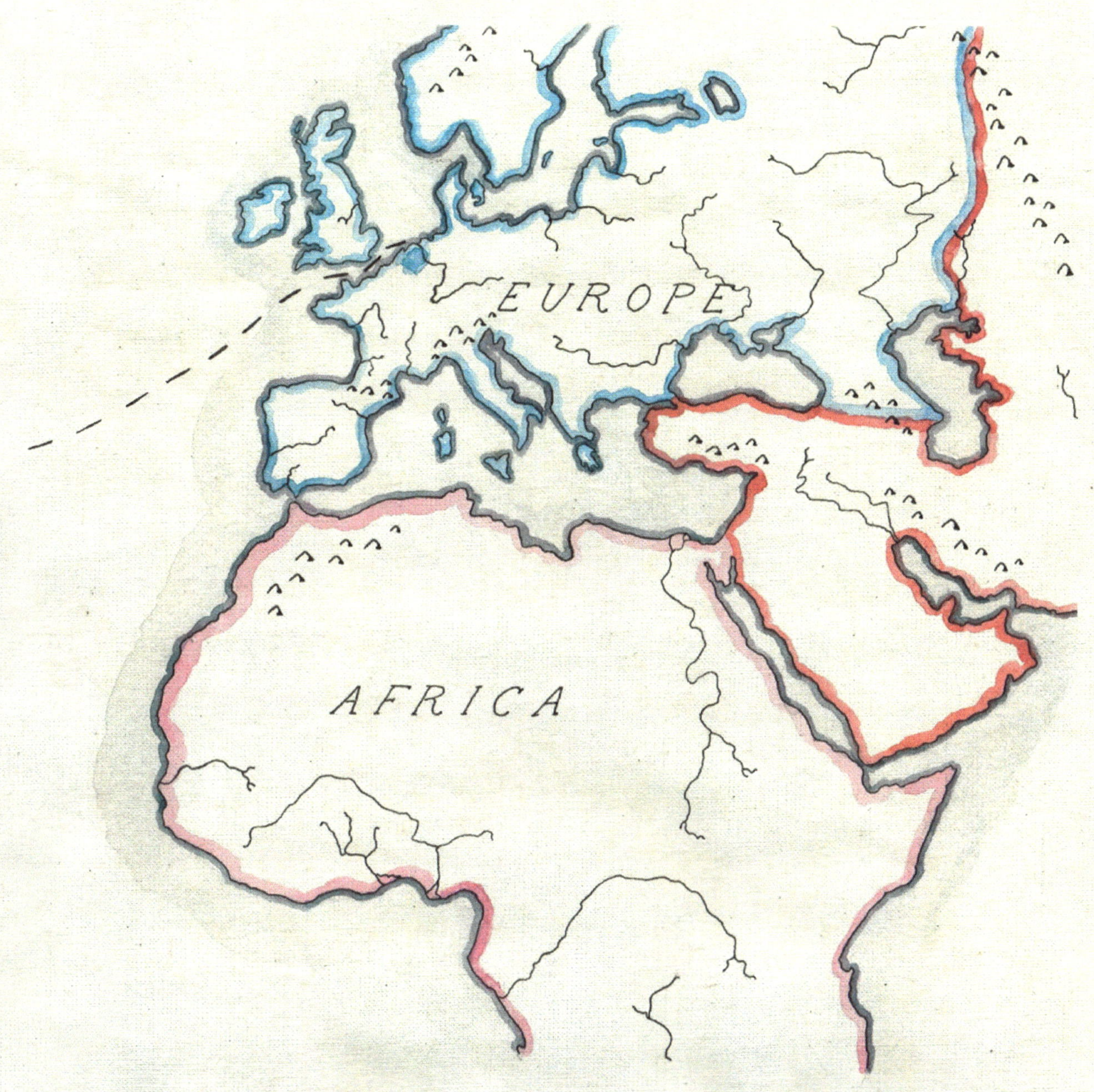

Maria left behind winter and cold. She left behind four dependable seasons. She sailed on a ship to Suriname, far, far away from anything she had ever known.

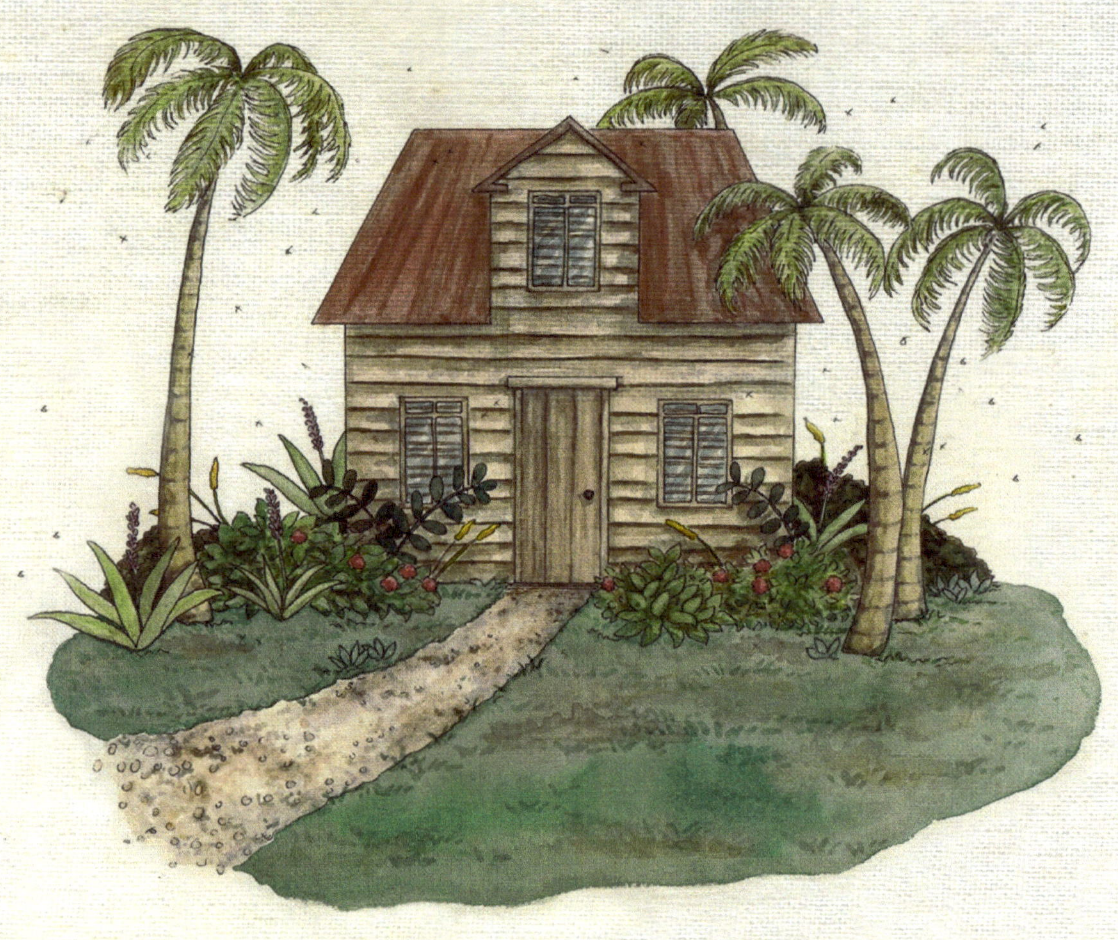

Maria emerged from the cramped
ship into thick, moist air and
the sounds of sailors yelling,
insects droning. She hauled
her trunks down crushed
seashell streets to a tiny
wooden house with a garden.

Maria pulled out her net and collecting jars and started to explore.

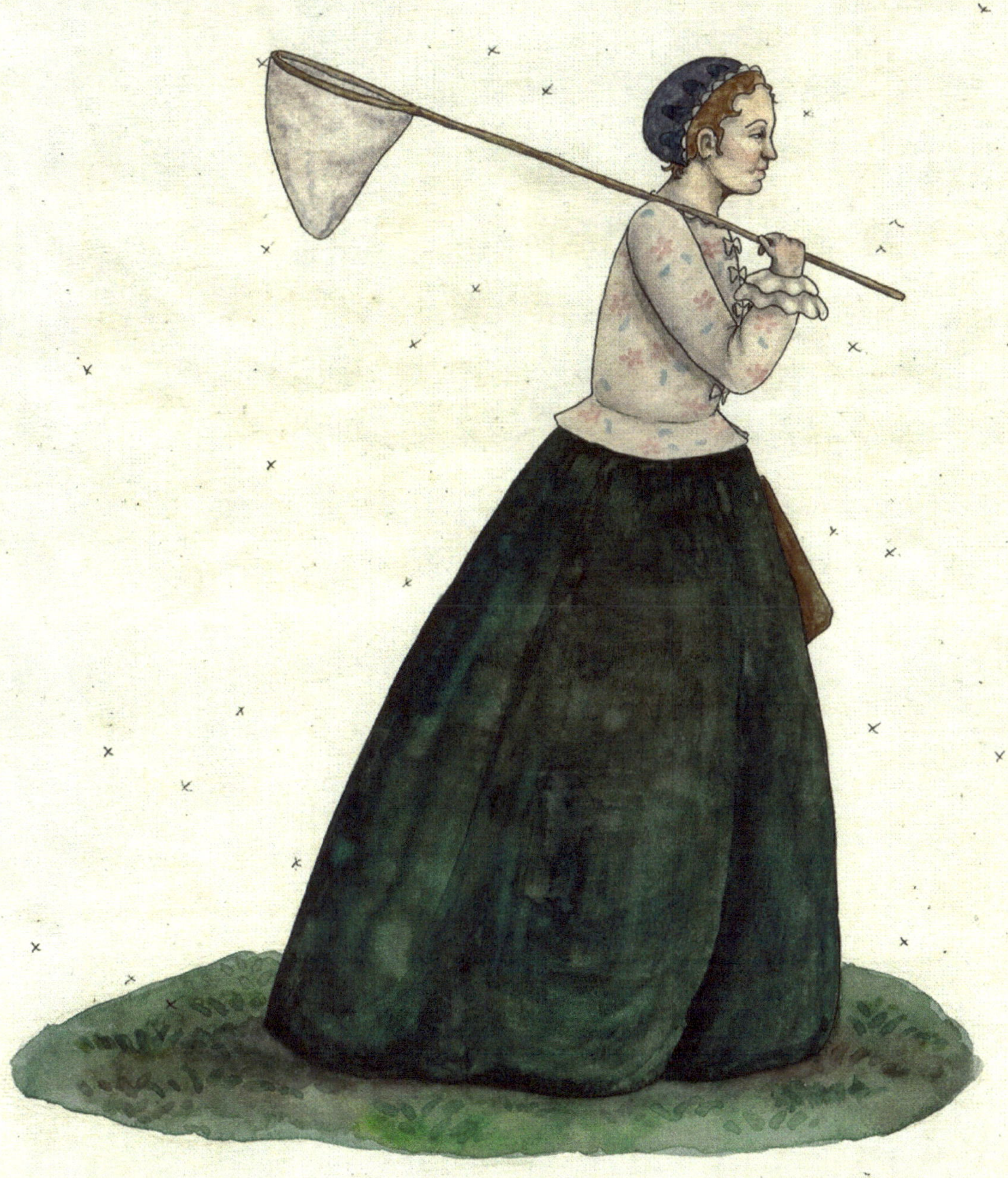

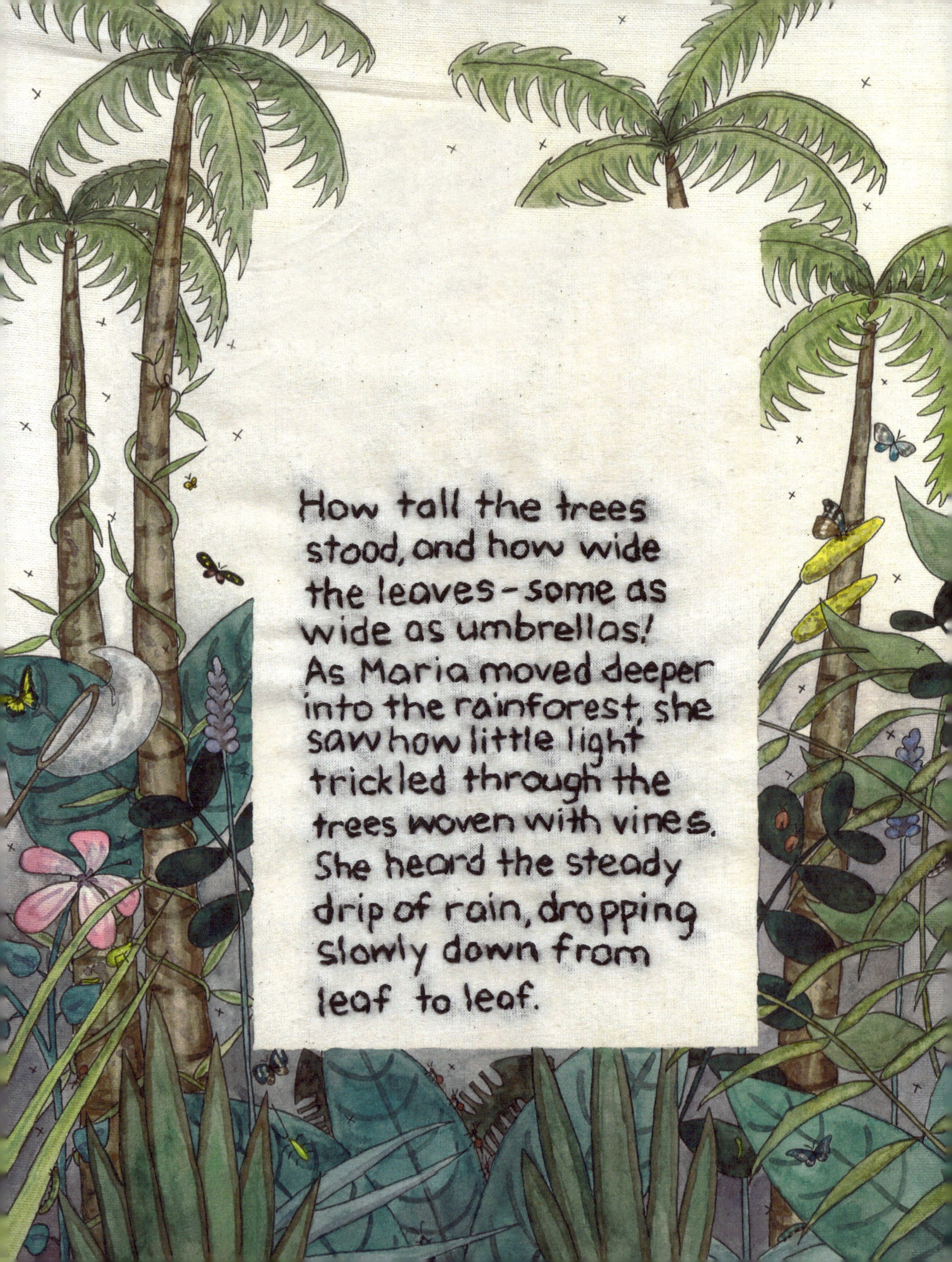

How tall the trees
stood, and how wide
the leaves - some as
wide as umbrellas!
As Maria moved deeper
into the rainforest, she
saw how little light
trickled through the
trees woven with vines.
She heard the steady
drip of rain, dropping
slowly down from
leaf to leaf.

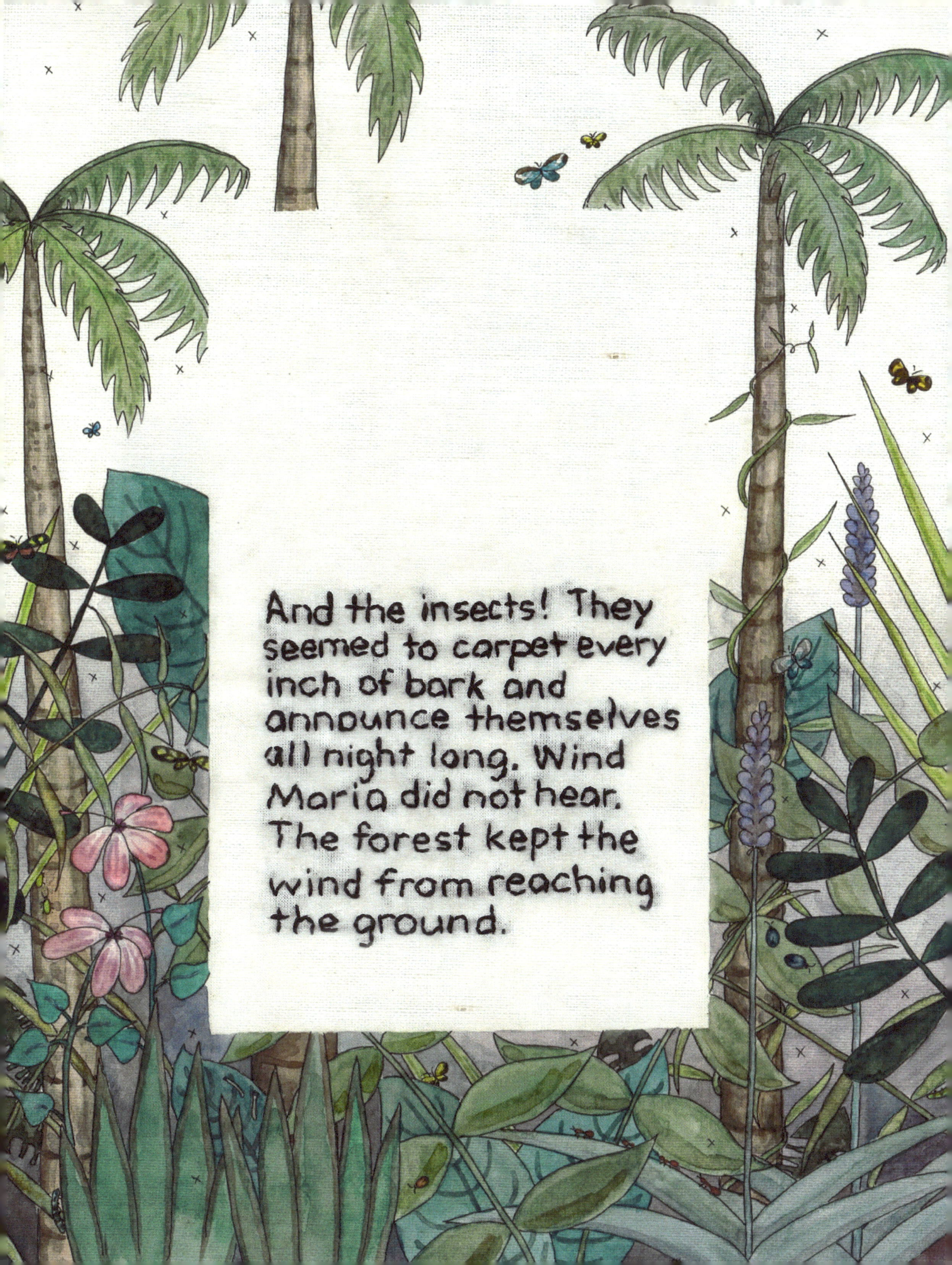

And the insects! They seemed to carpet every inch of bark and announce themselves all night long. Wind Maria did not hear. The forest kept the wind from reaching the ground.

Maria wore heavy clothes that tore
as she pushed through thorny
branches. Insects stung her
arms and neck. Her dress stuck
to her skin through the heat of
each day.

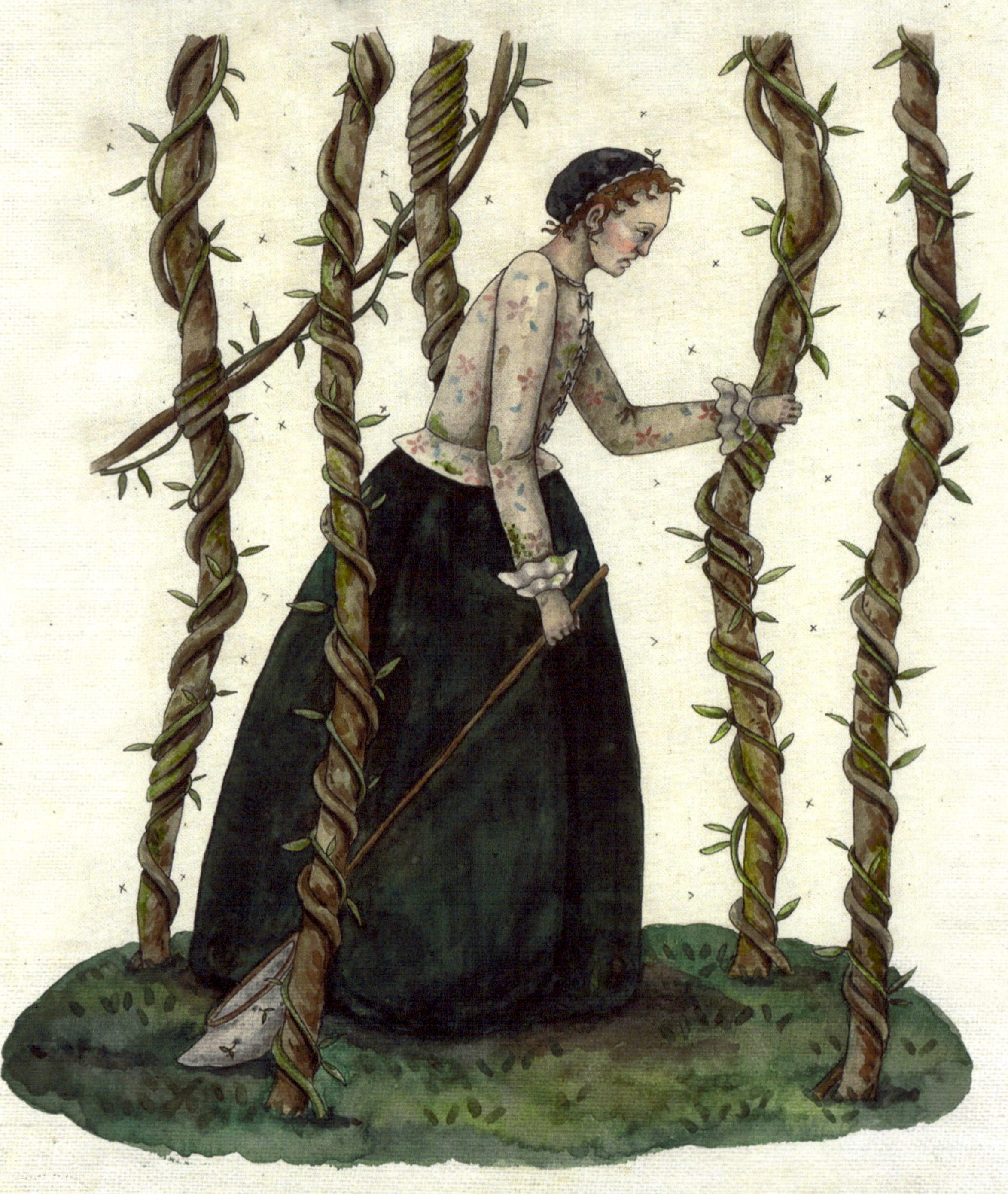

Maria found caterpillars that
died before she could figure out
what to feed them. She found
butterflies but never discovered
their caterpillars. It rained
for months at a time when
she could collect nothing at
all.

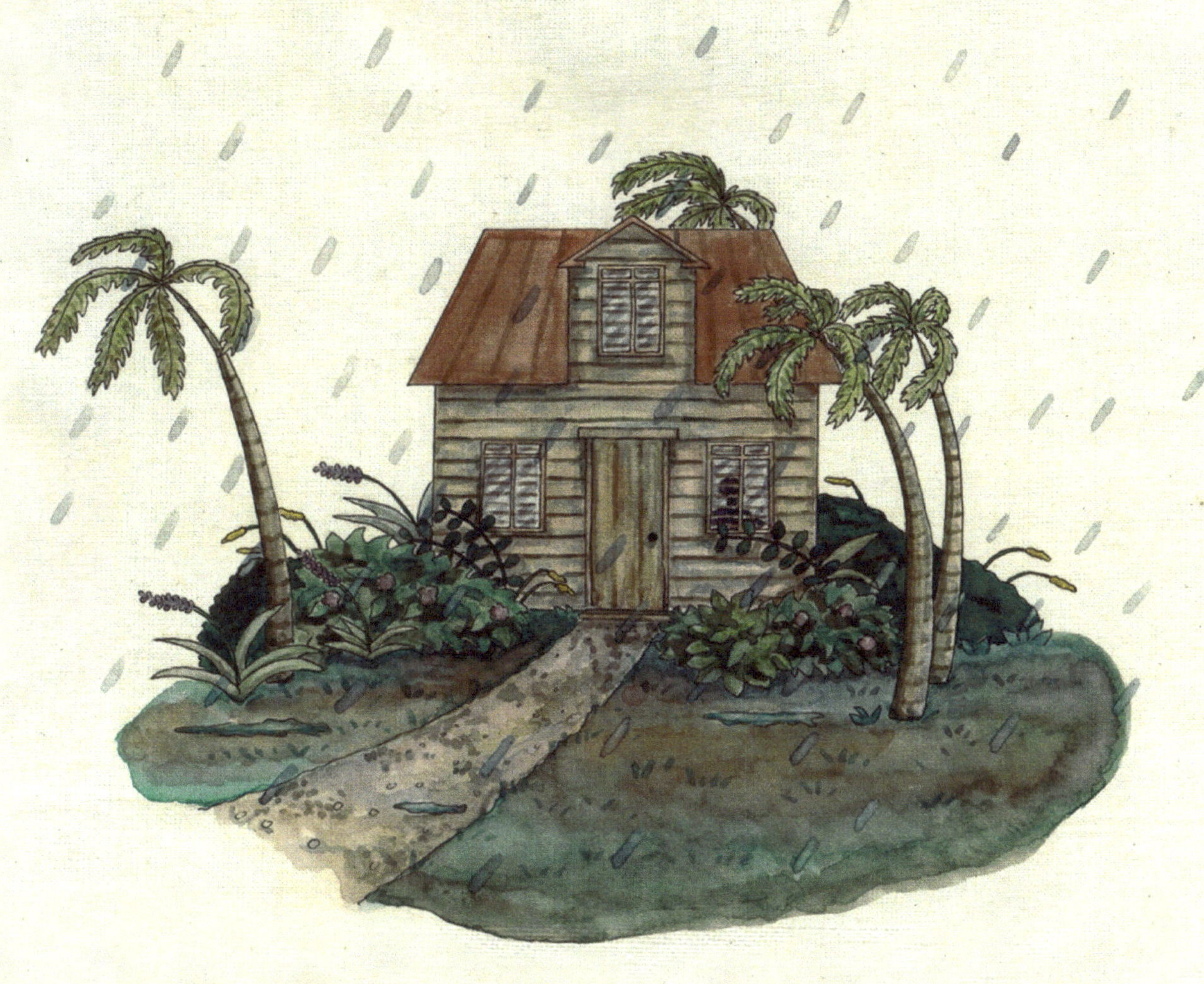

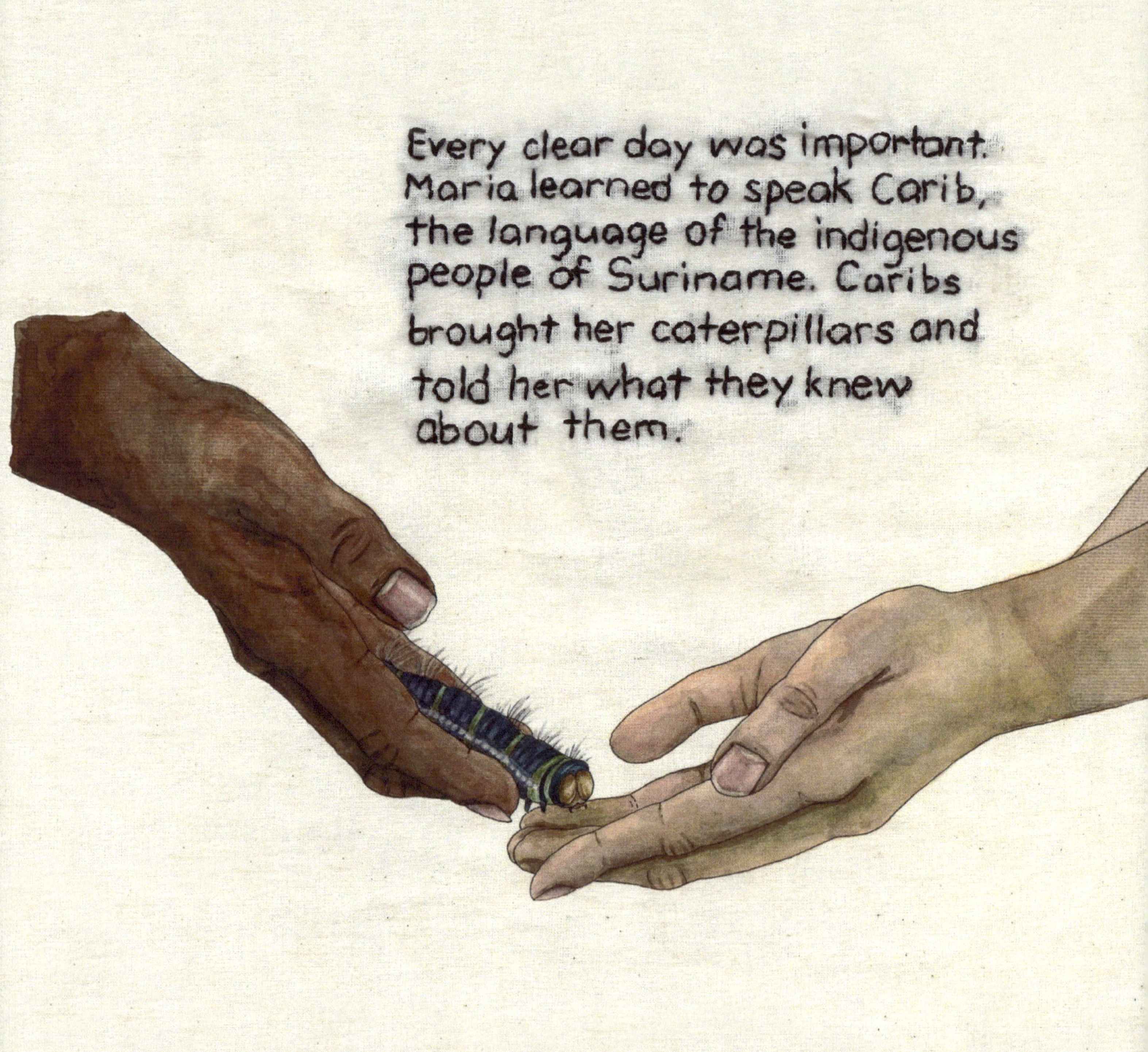

Every clear day was important. Maria learned to speak Carib, the language of the indigenous people of Suriname. Caribs brought her caterpillars and told her what they knew about them.

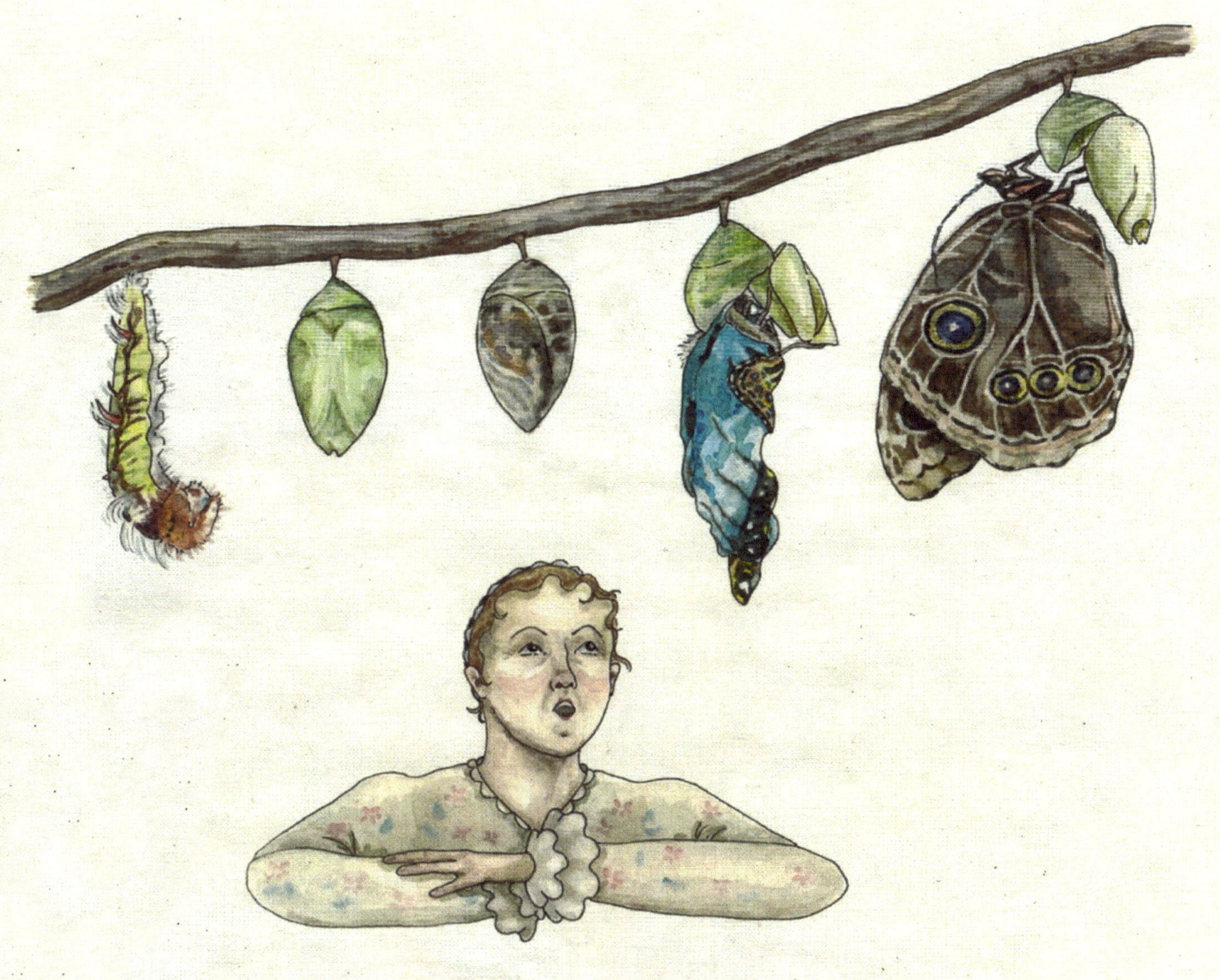

Every time a butterfly emerged
from its chrysalis, Maria held
her breath in wonder: what
would its wings look like on
top? What pattern would they
have underneath?

Maria could not paint as fast as she collected. She preserved specimens to paint during the rainy season or to take back to Amsterdam. She stayed in Suriname for two years. Then Maria became sick and needed to go home.

It was time to leave behind the
red-brown water of the river,
the steam off the river at
dawn, the pineapples growing
like weeds, and the ever-present
leafcutter ants that marched
in lines and carried puzzle
pieces of leaf bits.

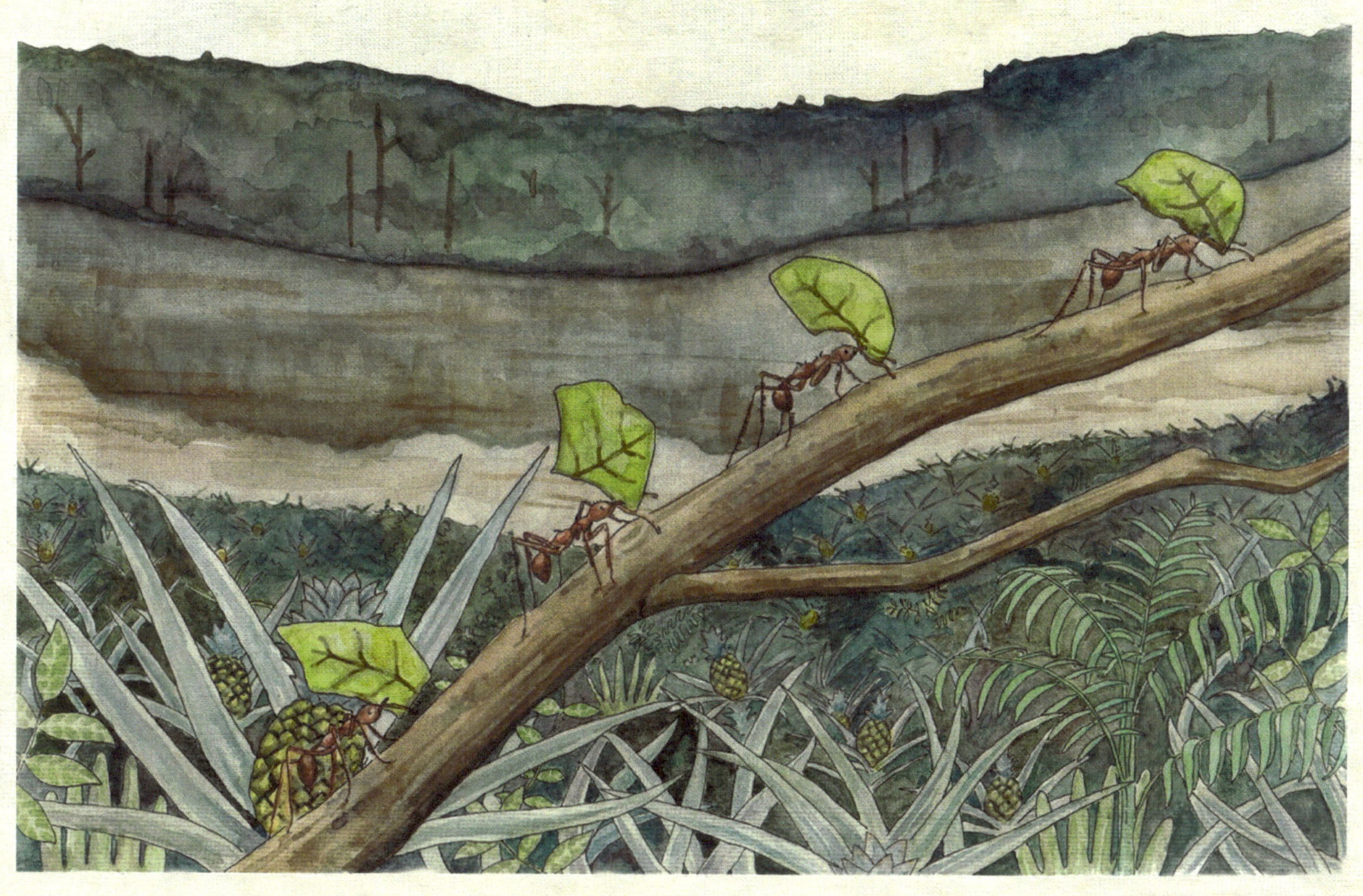

It was time to go home and create her dream.

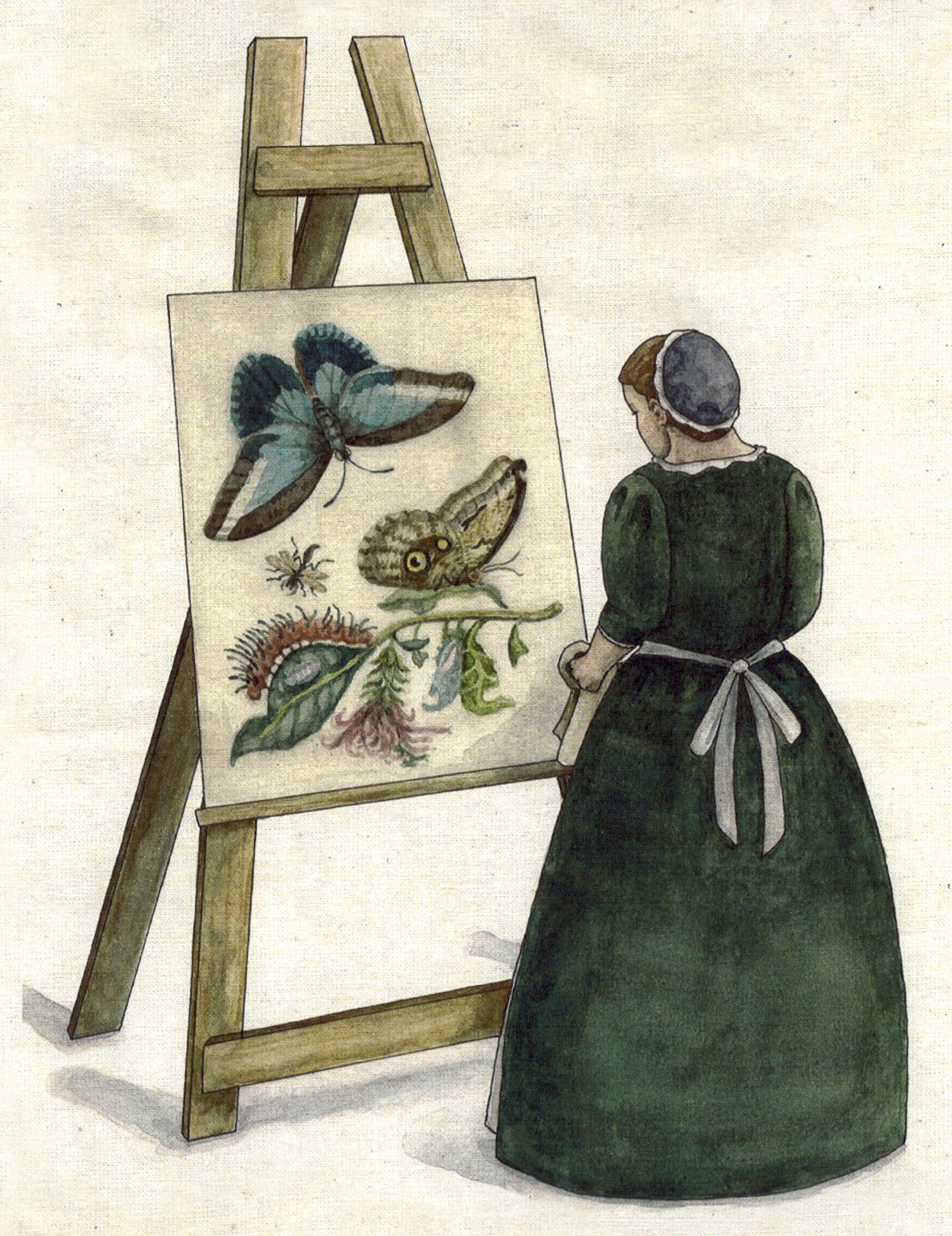

Maria drew and painted for
three years. Her paintings
were more vivid than any
she had created before.
They were more precise than
any drawings yet seen of
the Americas.

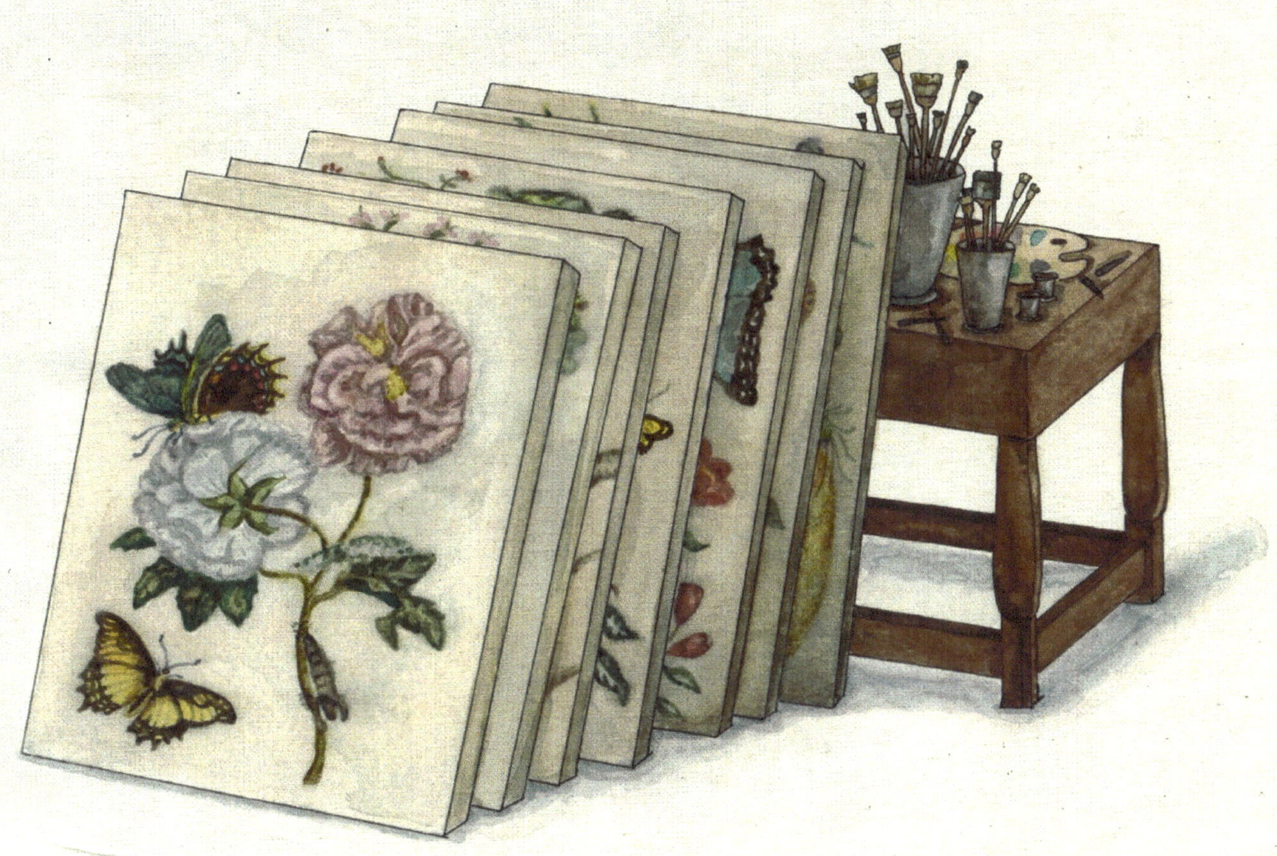

Publishing her book was not easy. Maria had to find subscribers, people who paid in advance for a copy of her book. She sold many of the specimens that she brought back to raise money. Maria painted pictures of people's collections to raise money.

Finally, in 1705, the <u>Suriname Insect Book</u> was published. Maria's paintings astounded people. Her art inspired others to travel to the Americas.

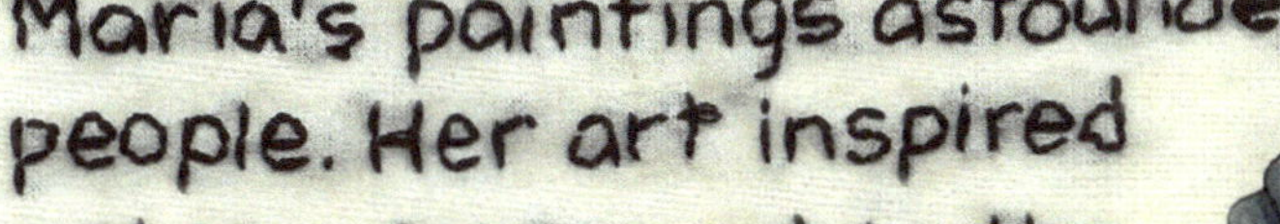

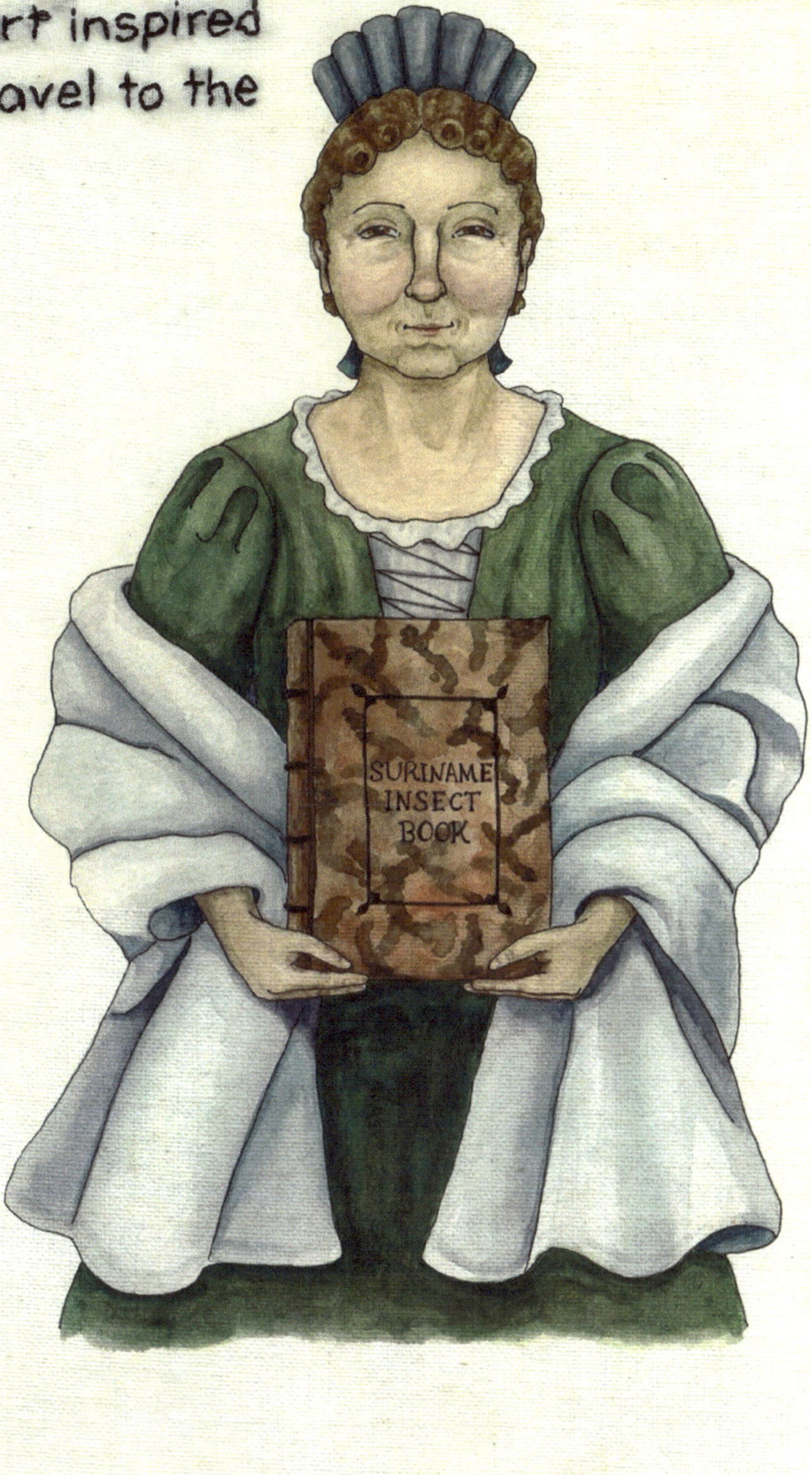

Scientists and artists bought
Maria's book. They marveled
at her idea. She painted
insects with the plants they
ate, something no one had
thought to do before. She
had crossed an ocean to
paint exactly what she saw.

Maria's paintings opened
a window to her readers.
Her butterflies flew in.

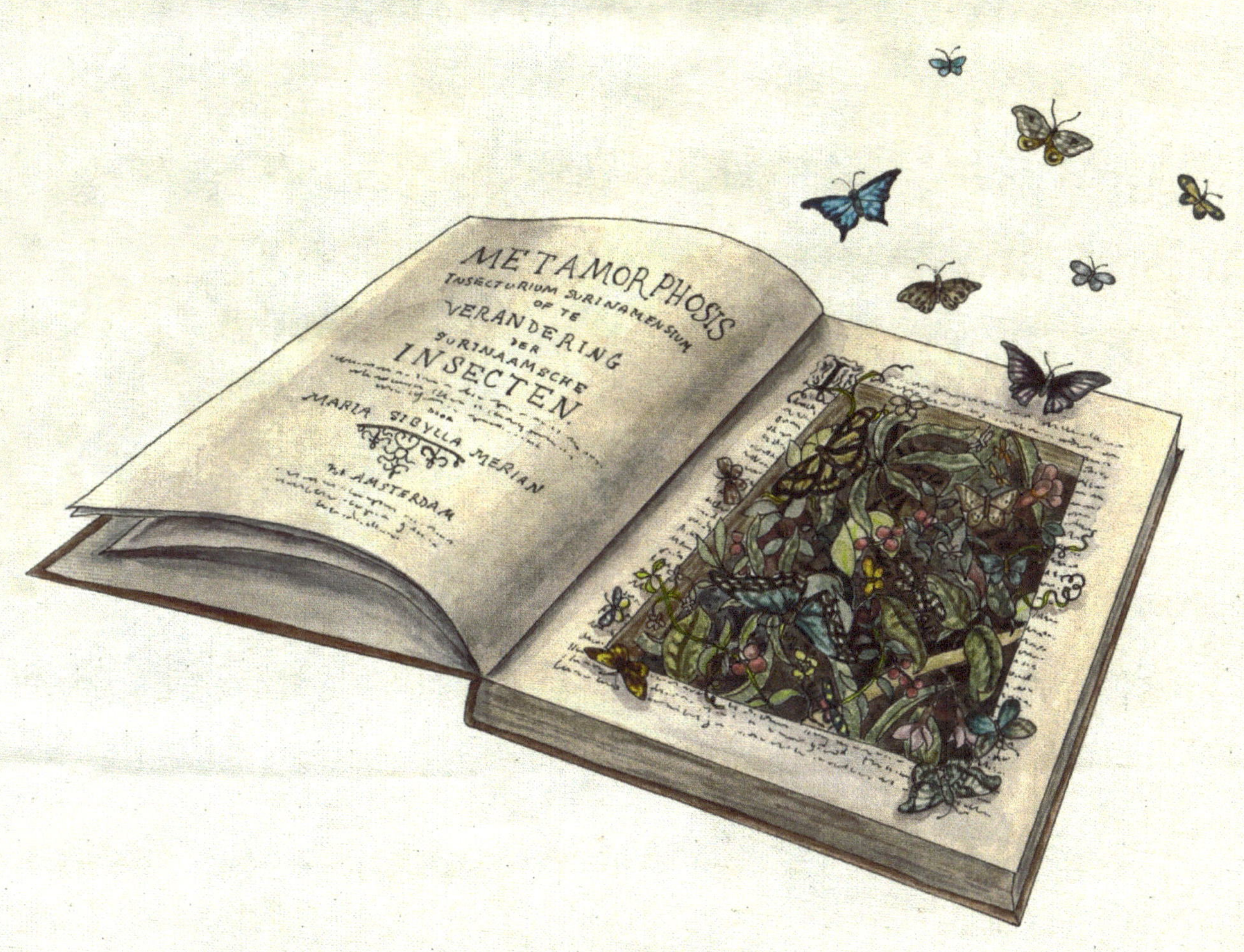

Maria Sibylla Merian was born in Frankfurt, Germany on April 2, 1647. Her father was a respected printer who died when she was three. Her stepfather was a painter who encouraged Maria to draw and paint. During her lifetime, she painted flowers, gave drawing lessons, created embroidery designs, and studied insects, frogs, and other creatures. Her detailed drawings helped scientists understand metamorphosis. Maria published three books of her paintings. She died in Amsterdam on January 13, 1717.

Paige Menton is a gardener, teacher, and poet. She founded Journeywork, an organization that restores land for caterpillars and other creatures.

Samantha Holden is a student at Ursinus College where she is majoring in biology and minoring in art. She has been watercolor painting for several years and drawing for many more. She was homeschooled and raised at the intersection of the artistic and natural worlds whose connections continue to inspire her.